Contents

Some words are shown in bold, **like this**. You can find out what they mean by looking in the glossary.

An Introduction to California

In the United States, any traveler moving west eventually ends up in California. The only state west of California is Hawaii, a group of islands in the Pacific Ocean. A person heading south from California will cross the border into the country of Mexico.

Alaska and Texas cover more land than California, but no state has more people. California is crowded because people have come to the state in such large numbers for so long. Four of the 20 biggest cities in the United States—Los Angeles, San Diego, San Jose, and San Francisco—are in California. However, some areas, such as Modoc County in the northeast, are nearly empty.

Once you reach the Pacific Ocean coast, you are at the edge of the United States. According to the U.S. Census Bureau data, over 36 million people lived in this warm, sunny state in 2006.

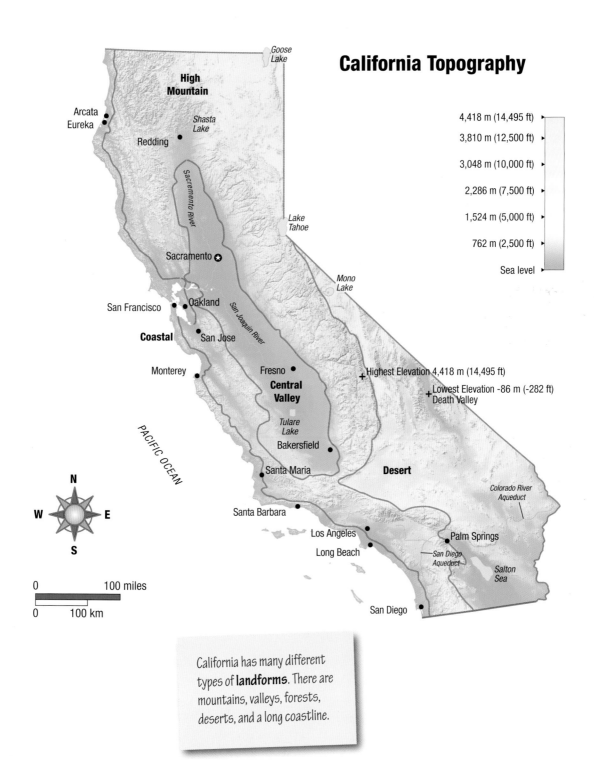

California Topography

Elevation	
4,418 m (14,495 ft)	▸
3,810 m (12,500 ft)	▸
3,048 m (10,000 ft)	▸
2,286 m (7,500 ft)	▸
1,524 m (5,000 ft)	▸
762 m (2,500 ft)	▸
Sea level	▸

Goose Lake

High Mountain

Arcata
Eureka

Shasta Lake

Redding

Sacramento River

Lake Tahoe

Sacramento ✪

Mono Lake

San Francisco • Oakland

San Joaquin River

Coastal • San Jose

Monterey

Fresno • Highest Elevation 4,418 m (14,495 ft)

Central Valley

+ Lowest Elevation -86 m (-282 ft)
Death Valley

Tulare Lake

Bakersfield

Santa Maria **Desert**

Colorado River Aqueduct

Santa Barbara

Los Angeles • Palm Springs

Long Beach

San Diego Aqueduct

Salton Sea

San Diego

PACIFIC OCEAN

N
W — E
S

0	100 miles
0	100 km

California has many different types of **landforms**. There are mountains, valleys, forests, deserts, and a long coastline.

Travel and **tourism** are big businesses throughout the state of California. Each year, more than 50 million tourists come in from other states and countries. More than one million Californians work in businesses that serve tourists. They drive tour buses, run restaurants and hotels, sell **souvenirs** and supplies, operate travel agencies, and so on. Tourism is worth $75 billion to the state each year, ranking as the third-largest state **industry**.

Earthquake Country

California sits on two great sheets of rock called plates. These plates float on a deeper layer of melted rock. Since the plates are separate, they can slip against each other. When they do, earthquakes jolt the ground above. California gets about 5,000 earthquakes each year. Most are too small to notice, but a few have been the biggest in U.S. history.

Mount San Jacinto and other snow-capped mountains are the background for the palm trees found in Palm Desert.

The Land that is California

When looking at California from above, you would find it divided among several landforms. Tall mountains line the northern border of the state and much of the eastern border. Lower mountain ranges wrinkle the land along the West Coast. Between the Coast Ranges and the Sierra Nevada range in the east lies a long, slipper-shaped plain called the Central Valley. There are also three neighboring deserts: the Mojave Desert, Death Valley, and the Colorado Desert.

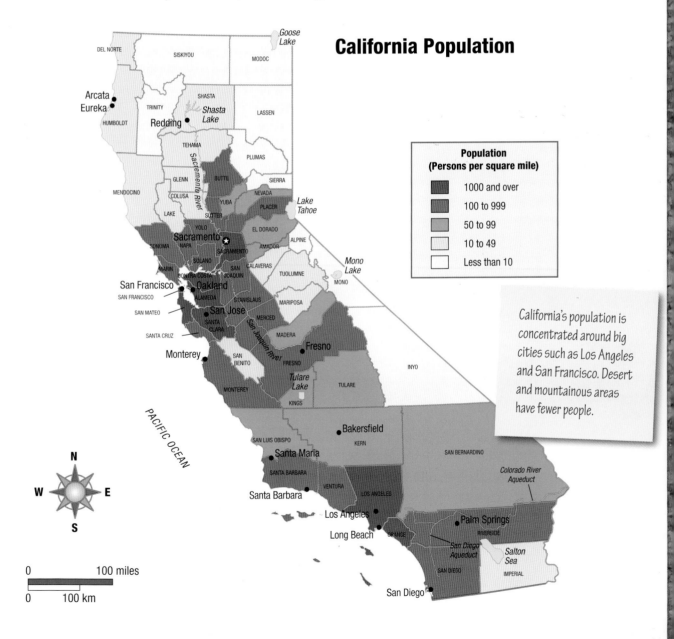

California Population

Population (Persons per square mile)

- 1000 and over
- 100 to 999
- 50 to 99
- 10 to 49
- Less than 10

California's population is concentrated around big cities such as Los Angeles and San Francisco. Desert and mountainous areas have fewer people.

The California Economy

Gross Domestic Product in 2007 (in dollars)

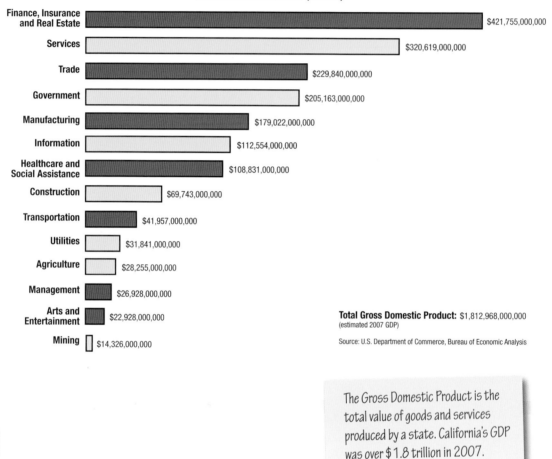

Finance, Insurance and Real Estate	$421,755,000,000
Services	$320,619,000,000
Trade	$229,840,000,000
Government	$205,163,000,000
Manufacturing	$179,022,000,000
Information	$112,554,000,000
Healthcare and Social Assistance	$108,831,000,000
Construction	$69,743,000,000
Transportation	$41,957,000,000
Utilities	$31,841,000,000
Agriculture	$28,255,000,000
Management	$26,928,000,000
Arts and Entertainment	$22,928,000,000
Mining	$14,326,000,000

Total Gross Domestic Product: $1,812,968,000,000
(estimated 2007 GDP)

Source: U.S. Department of Commerce, Bureau of Economic Analysis

> The Gross Domestic Product is the total value of goods and services produced by a state. California's GDP was over $1.8 trillion in 2007.

Each region in California is unique. Each faces different challenges in meeting the needs of its population. Each region has varied landforms that affect the people who live there. Different industries employ many types of workers, and each region also offers different **recreational** opportunities as well. Cities are the heart of some regions, while vast, open spaces are found in others. Together, all of these regions create a state that is appealing to people of all ages and **ethnicities**. This state is California.

The Northern Coast

The land of the California coast varies from north to south. North of San Luis Obispo, the coast becomes more rugged. High hills rise directly from the water's edge. Narrow beaches are tucked between the hills, and big rocks rise out of the waters offshore. Barking seals and squawking gulls cover these rocks. Big Sur, the over 97 kilometers (60 miles) of land between San Luis Obispo and Monterey Bay, is the most rugged part of the California coastline.

Climate

The weather on the north coast is cool, but never bitterly cold. Light snow may dust the mountaintops at times, but that's all. The rainfall increases, too. Del Norte, the most northern county, gets an average of 1.5 meters (60.5 inches) a year. San Francisco's average summer temperatures are in the low 70s, yet winter temperatures rarely fall below freezing 0° Celsius (32° Fahrenheit).

In the central and north coast regions, mountain ranges run along the 2,034-kilometer (1,264-mile) coastline.

Farming

The north coast has many natural **resources** important to farmers. The valleys that cut through the coast range have excellent soil. This part of the coast also gets plenty of rain. North of Santa Cruz, fields of asparagus and other vegetables are visible from the road. North of San Francisco, many dairy farms produce eggs, milk, and cheese. The small city of Petaluma calls itself the egg **capital** of the world.

California Coastal Topography

Elevation
4,418 m (14,495 ft) ▸
3,810 m (12,500 ft) ▸
3,048 m (10,000 ft) ▸
2,286 m (7,500 ft) ▸
1,524 m (5,000 ft) ▸
762 m (2,500 ft) ▸
Sea level ▸

Oregon
Goose Lake
High Mountain
Arcata
Eureka
Shasta Lake
Redding
Sacramento River
Coastal
Lake Tahoe
Sacramento
San Pablo Bay
San Francisco
San Francisco Bay
Oakland
Mono Lake
San Jose
San Joaquin River
Monterey Bay
Monterey
Fresno
Central Valley
Highest Elevation 4,418 m (14,495)
Lowest Elevation -86 m (-282 ft.)
Death Valley
Big Sur area
PACIFIC OCEAN
Tulare Lake
Bakersfield
San Luis Obispo
Santa Maria
Desert
Santa Barbara
Colorado River Aqueduct
Los Angeles
Palm Springs
Santa Barbara islands
Long Beach
San Diego Aqueduct
Salton Sea
Catalina Island
San Diego
San Diego Bay
MEXICO

The rocky and mountainous coast of California was formed by natural forces such as volcanoes and earthquakes.

N
W E
S

0   100 miles
0   100 km

The richest "farms" of coastal California **thrive** in the Napa and Sonoma Valleys. Almost all of these "farms" are **vineyards**. At one time, almost all of America's fine wines came from Napa Valley. Later, Sonoma began to rival Napa. Now, many states have wineries, but the wines from Sonoma and Napa still win many prizes.

Fishers catch king salmon on the north coast, a fish prized for its sweet meat. Divers may only gather abalone in the north, from San Francisco to the state line. This tasty shellfish is decreasing in population. People need a special fishing license to catch them.

Grapes grown in California are used not only for wine, but to make raisins and be sold as fruit for eating.

Northern California is considered the salmon capital of the West Coast. Here, a fishing boat brings in the day's catch.

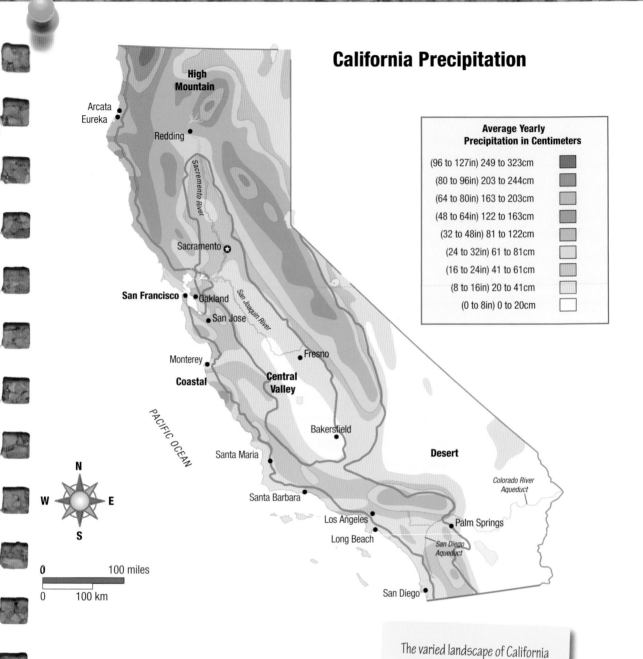

California Precipitation

High Mountain

Arcata
Eureka

Redding

Sacramento River

Sacramento

San Francisco
Oakland
San Jose

San Joaquin River

Monterey

Fresno

Central Valley

Coastal

PACIFIC OCEAN

Bakersfield

Santa Maria

Desert

Santa Barbara

Colorado River Aqueduct

Los Angeles
Palm Springs

Long Beach
San Diego Aqueduct

San Diego

Average Yearly Precipitation in Centimeters

(96 to 127in) 249 to 323cm
(80 to 96in) 203 to 244cm
(64 to 80in) 163 to 203cm
(48 to 64in) 122 to 163cm
(32 to 48in) 81 to 122cm
(24 to 32in) 61 to 81cm
(16 to 24in) 41 to 61cm
(8 to 16in) 20 to 41cm
(0 to 8in) 0 to 20cm

N
W   E
S

0   100 miles
0   100 km

The varied landscape of California affects the amount of rain each area receives. The deserts get very little rain, while the northern region is often wet and rainy.

San Francisco

Crowded San Francisco covers one of the **peninsulas** that form the Golden Gate. It cannot grow larger because water surrounds it on three sides. Other cities, however, extend around the Bay. Each one merges into the next, with no real countryside in between. Berkeley sits across the Bay, east of San Francisco. It merges into Oakland in the south. Oakland gives way to a string of smaller cities. The **suburbs** of San Jose begin where the smaller cities end.

San Francisco grew up almost overnight during the gold rush of the late 1840s and early 1850s. Money still pours through it, because San Francisco is the financial center of the West Coast. The downtown area looks like a forest of banks. San Francisco is also an important **cultural** center. The city has the important Asian Art Museum, an opera company, a **symphony**, and a ballet.

Much of the city is built on steep hills that offer views of the ocean and bay. The San Francisco Bay is a huge bay on the West Coast and has a narrow mouth that makes it more like an **inland** sea. Two peninsulas form this mouth. Behind this mouth, the bay stretches both north and south. The northern branch is called the San Pablo Bay. The Sacramento River pours into the tip of it. The other branch, the San Francisco Bay, flows generally south about 97 kilometers (60 miles).

Almost every house that survived the 1906 earthquake has been **preserved**, giving San Francisco a charming, historic feel. Many of these wooden houses are called "Victorians" because their style took shape when Queen Victoria ruled Great Britain. Many houses have **gables**, **turrets**, and **bay windows**. They are often painted in bright colors to make the decorations stand out. San Francisco's beauty is an **economic** resource, too, because it draws tourists to the city.

Many of the neighborhoods in San Francisco have old Victorian homes like these. They are called "painted ladies" because of the beautiful detailing on them.

California Coastal Resources

Natural Resources

- Oil
- Natural gas
- Borax
- Limestone
- Gold, silver
- Sand, gravel

Manufacturing

- Computers
- Clothing

Industry

- Forest products
- Fruit
- Grapes
- Rice
- Vegetables
- Olives
- Dairy products
- Cotton
- Sugar beets
- Cattle
- Walnuts
- Poultry
- Fish
- Skiing

High Mountain

Arcata
Eureka

Redding

Sacramento

San Francisco · Oakland
Coastal · San Jose

PACIFIC OCEAN

Monterey

Fresno
Central Valley

Bakersfield

Santa Maria

Santa Barbara

Desert

Los Angeles
Long Beach

Palm Springs

San Diego

N W E S

0   100 miles
0   100 km

Tourist Attractions

San Francisco's interesting neighborhoods are also an economic resource. Chinatown, for example, has the look and feel of a city in China. North Beach is full of Italian restaurants and coffeehouses. A famous group of poets called the Beats lived and worked there in the 1950s. Tourists still come to San Francisco to relive the Beat Era. Haight Ashbury is another famous neighborhood. The hippie movement of the 1960s was born there. Haight Street still looks much as it did in that time.

The long coastal region provides many of California's resources, including fruits and vegetables, oil, forest products, and manufactured goods.

In the 1960s, Haight Ashbury was the center for music, painting, poetry, and literature.

Cable cars run along three of San Francisco's streets. They are used mainly by tourists. Other attractions include the Golden Gate Bridge and Golden Gate Park. Also, more than 14 million travelers visit the Golden Gate National **Recreation** Area. This is a set of parks and woods that stretches from San Francisco into Marin. It gets the most paid visitors of any national park in the state.

The San Francisco Bay Area

Several cities together make up the San Francisco Bay Area, the major **urban** center of the north. Berkeley revolves mainly around one **industry**, which is education. This town boasts the first and finest **campus** in the University of California system. Because of the university, a large number of the people in Berkeley are students.

Oakland, by contrast, is often seen as less interesting by its Bay Area neighbors. It too has the old houses and the beautiful views, but it is a working city filled with small factories. Oakland's waterfront remains a working port, not a tourist's playground.

A variety of fish wait for sale at the Stockton Street Fish Market in San Francisco.

San Jose is not as well known as San Francisco, but it actually has more people. It is the biggest city in the Bay Area. For many years, it served as a **hub** for the farms of the Central Valley. Now, San Jose has stronger ties to the Bay Area computer industry.

Northern California does not have as many people as the southern part of the state. However, it does have several state and national parks and opportunities for outdoor recreation, including hiking, camping, and fishing.

Northern California is probably best known as the home of Silicon Valley, in Santa Clara County. Most computer companies have main offices in Silicon Valley, the area between San Jose and San Francisco.

High-tech machines help make parts for computers and other machinery. Below are the headquarters for the Oracle Corporation, located in Silicon Valley.

Other Northern California industries include the largest **bioscience** industry in the world and several important entertainment studios as well. Many special effects that you see in movies are made at Marin County's Industrial Light and Magic.

The Bay Area has many public transportation systems. Each city has its own bus system. Some commuters take ferries to San Francisco. They must then board a bus to get to their destination. Others ride the Bay Area Rapid Transit, also known as BART. Another system called Caltrans runs trains to the south Bay. The Golden Gate Transit runs buses to Marin. Amtrak trains stop in Oakland, and they carry passengers to and from distant cities. Most visitors, however, arrive by car or fly into one of the Bay Area's three airports.

Bay Area Rapid Transit (BART) mainly connects downtown San Francisco to cities and suburbs east of the Bay.

The Southern Coast

The Monterey Bay National Marine Sanctuary is a federally protected offshore marine area on California's central coast. It is home to fish, mammals, plants, invertebrates, and seabirds.

The southern coast is marked by long stretches of flat, sandy beach. A number of large islands, including the Santa Barbara Islands and Catalina Island, lie offshore. Set back from the beaches are rolling hills. These hills rise to mountain ranges.

Two large bays cut into the southern coast of California. Near the Mexican border is the San Diego Bay. It is a deep, narrow channel shaped like a candy cane. North of Big Sur is Monterey Bay, a wide curve shaped like a crescent moon. It is located about halfway between Mexico and the state of Oregon.

Climate

Southwestern California has a Mediterranean **climate**. This means that rain falls only in the winter and the temperature is mild. Summers are warm but rarely get unpleasantly hot, because ocean breezes help to cool things off. Winters never get very cold. Storms drench the coast at times, but the rain falls in short, heavy bursts. Southern California gets more days of sunshine than most of the world—over 300 days a year.

The climate of southern California is very pleasant, but it has created a problem, too. It has attracted too many people for the amount of water available. Rivers in southern California usually run dry in the summer.

Gravity pulls water through the aqueducts, over the hills of California, supplying water to the Los Angeles area.

A Dry Area

The most important waterways are those made by people: long **canals** called **aqueducts**. The Los Angeles Aqueduct brings water from the Owens Valley in the Sierra Nevada. The Colorado Aqueduct brings water from the Colorado River. Near Los Angeles, the aqueduct branches into two waterways. One branch runs south to San Diego. Without aqueducts, the south coast would have very few people.

The south coast is too dry for most crops, but citrus fruits can **thrive** there. These fruits include lemons, oranges, and grapefruit. America's first navel oranges were grown along the coast in the early 1870s. Later, a California grower developed the Valencia orange, which ripens in summer and fall. Since navel oranges ripen in winter, California could then produce citrus crops year-round. The area south of Los Angeles came to be called Orange County because it produced so many oranges.

Today, Orange County has only a few orange groves. Many farms did not survive because too many people wanted to live in the area.

As the value of land increased, many citrus growers decided to sell their farms. They moved north and east of Los Angeles, to Kern County and beyond. California still produces a great deal of citrus fruit. However, in Orange County, housing **developments** have replaced orange groves.

A tugboat guides a container ship through the San Pedro Harbor.

Fishing

California has rich **resources** in the sea, which borders the state's entire coast. The waters of the Pacific Ocean are full of fish and shellfish. Most of the catch is brought in by people who catch fish for money. Some of them work for big companies. Others are part of family-owned businesses.

The boats sail from ports in San Diego, Long Beach, Los Angeles, Santa Barbara, and San Luis Obispo. Fishers often use nets to capture fish by the ton. Some boats stay at sea for months, storing the fish on ice to keep them fresh.

California's biggest moneymaker now is **sea urchin**. Much of this catch is sold to Japan. There, people like the taste of it in sushi—a dish made of rice, seaweed, and raw fish.

Large numbers of anchovies are still harvested from the ocean. Anchovies measure only a few inches, but they run in **schools** of millions. Because of their strong flavor, anchovies are used more like a spice than a food. Tons of anchovies are also ground up and made into **fertilizer** or animal feed every year.

Ocean Resources

The ocean also supplies an important **mineral** resource—petroleum. Oil was first found in California on land that is now Los Angeles. When the oil wells ran dry, more oil was found offshore. Today, oil companies work from platforms out in the ocean. They pump oil from beneath the ocean floor. When they find oil or petroleum, they usually find a type of natural gas, too. This gas is the kind you might use as fuel for a camp stove.

Oil is found in sedimentary rock beneath the ocean floor.

The black goo that comes out of the ground is crude oil. It goes to nearby **refineries**, which separate the goo into useful products. Heating oil, petroleum jelly, plastic, and, above all, gasoline, are all made from crude oil.

California uses all the oil it produces and even buys more from other states and countries. California uses a great deal of energy because it is such a busy place. It produces more manufactured goods than any other state.

Southern California Industries

California factories make airplanes and airplane parts, spaceships, missiles, and weapons. They make medical equipment and scientific instruments. They make electronic goods such as video recorders and computers.

Los Angeles has a large clothing **industry**. Most of the actual sewing is done in Mexico and other countries. Southern California workers **design** the clothes, model them, advertise them, and handle the business details.

Many of these jobs take years of technical training. The training is provided by private and public colleges and universities. The great private schools include the California Institute of Technology (Caltech), Stanford University, and the University of Southern California. The University of California is one of the public universities. It has **campuses** in Los Angeles, Davis, Santa Cruz, Berkeley, and six other cities.

Rodeo Drive in Beverly Hills is a tourist attraction known for its designer clothing stores.

Entertainment

One of the biggest industries in California is entertainment. Los Angeles is the **capital** of this industry in the United States. It is home to actors, directors, writers, performers, singers, and artists of every kind. It also has many workers with technical skills, such as camera operators and sound **engineers**. Most movies and many TV shows are made in southern California. From Los Angeles to San Francisco, there are many music recording studios, too.

Theme parks are another **profitable** entertainment business. Disney Studios started the trend with Disneyland **Resort**. Universal Studios followed with its movie park. Today, California has dozens of theme parks.

Many people move to California to "make it big" in Hollywood. The entertainment industry is huge in the state.

The Myth of Hollywood

"Hollywood movies" are not really made in Hollywood anymore, but in other parts of Los Angeles. The real Hollywood was a small town where the movie industry was born. Now, it's a run-down neighborhood in Los Angeles that is slowly being **restored**.

Los Angeles has 16 major highways and about a dozen lesser ones that run throughout the city.

Los Angeles

About one-third of all Californians live in the Los Angeles area. Los Angeles is the biggest city on the West Coast and the second biggest in the country. The city itself stretches 80.5 kilometers (50 miles) from north to south, and it has no clear boundaries. Los Angeles blends into Long Beach, which blends into the next city to the south, and so on. From any hilltop you can see sheets of one- or two-story buildings stretching over the horizon.

Most big cities have a crowded downtown area surrounded by more quiet neighborhoods. Los Angeles does not. Offices, factories, and businesses are found throughout the city. Los Angeles is really a collection of neighborhoods sewn together by freeways. Each neighborhood has its own busy sections. A few even have their own governments. Los Angeles has been called "a hundred **suburbs** in search of a city," but that is not really correct. Los Angeles has world-class attractions similar to those of cities like New York, like big-league sports teams, important museums, and famous universities.

Los Angeles is a **diverse** city. People of many different **ethnic** groups live throughout the city. Some neighborhoods are especially known for an ethnic community. The *barrio* in east Los Angeles is largely **Latino**. Many African Americans live in Watts. The city also has large Filipino, Japanese, Chinese, and Korean neighborhoods.

Despite its wealth and importance, Los Angeles has serious problems. It has no subway system and the bus system is very limited. It is difficult to get around the city without cars. Freeways fill the landscape—and yet the freeways are often jammed. The many cars produce a lot of air pollution.

On hot days, the mountains around Los Angeles trap the polluted air. It mixes with fog and becomes smog, a thick, yellow air that is hard to breathe.

San Diego

The city of San Diego feels like a small town compared to Los Angeles. Actually, to the surprise of many, it ranks as the seventh largest city in the United States. Tourists flock to San Diego for the fine weather, clean air, warm ocean, and big surf.

Gigantic Balboa Park, in the middle of San Diego, contains a famous zoo with 800 **species** of animals on display. What makes this zoo special is the place itself. Animals do not live in cages, but in large areas built to look like their homes in nature. More than 3 million visitors to the zoo each year bring a lot of money into San Diego.

The military adds a great deal to the **economy** of this city as well. San Diego Bay is one of the world's great natural harbors. It is deep, and a long, skinny **peninsula** protects it from the ocean. That is why the country's largest naval base, San Diego Naval Base, is located here.

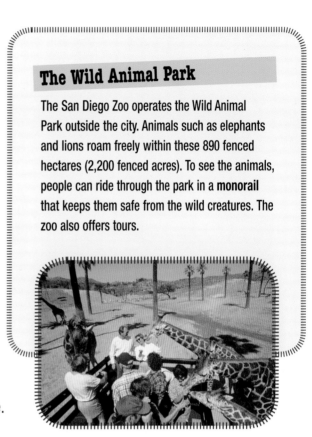

The Wild Animal Park

The San Diego Zoo operates the Wild Animal Park outside the city. Animals such as elephants and lions roam freely within these 890 fenced hectares (2,200 fenced acres). To see the animals, people can ride through the park in a **monorail** that keeps them safe from the wild creatures. The zoo also offers tours.

Sunny days, warm water, and sandy beaches make surfing a popular sport.

California Transportation

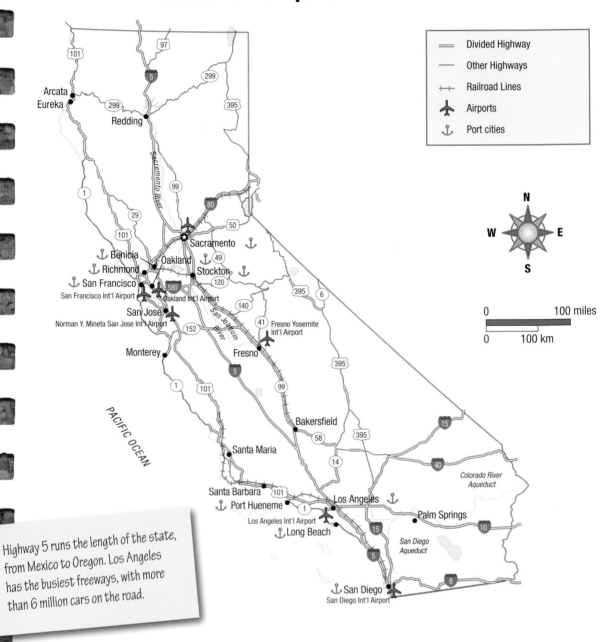

Legend:
- Divided Highway
- Other Highways
- Railroad Lines
- Airports
- Port cities

Arcata
Eureka
Redding
Benicia
Richmond
Oakland
San Francisco
San Francisco Int'l Airport
Oakland Int'l Airport
Sacramento
Stockton
San Jose
Norman Y. Mineta San Jose Int'l Airport
Monterey
Fresno
Fresno Yosemite Int'l Airport
Bakersfield
Santa Maria
Santa Barbara
Port Hueneme
Los Angeles
Los Angeles Int'l Airport
Long Beach
Palm Springs
San Diego
San Diego Int'l Airport
Colorado River Aqueduct
San Diego Aqueduct
PACIFIC OCEAN
Sacramento River
San Joaquin River

Highway 5 runs the length of the state, from Mexico to Oregon. Los Angeles has the busiest freeways, with more than 6 million cars on the road.

Coming and Going

Ships, trains, planes, and cars carry people and goods to and from California. San Pedro port in Los Angeles is the busiest port in the United States and the third busiest in the world. Oakland is a busy port as well. Through these and other California ports, goods flow to and from Asia. Cargo flows across the Mexican border, too, carried by trucks and trains. California leads the nation in the value of its trade.

The Central Valley

California's Central Valley is a great plain, 644 kilometers (400 miles) long and 80.5 kilometers (50 miles) wide. On a clear day, from the flat floor of the valley, you can see mountains on either side. The Sierra Nevada Mountains loom in the east like jagged teeth. In the west, you can see the gentle coastal hills. Within the valley, only a few peaks poke up here and there. They are the remains of ancient volcanoes.

Drive in any direction, however, and you come at last to hills. In the north, these hills mark the beginning of the Klamath range. In the south, the Tehachapi Mountains close the valley as they join with the curving tip of the Sierra Nevada. In short, mountains form a ring around the Central Valley.

In a **basin** like the Central Valley, water often forms salty lakes because it has nowhere to go. The Central Valley, however, has a drain. Its waters pour into the sea through one gap in the coast range—the San Francisco Bay.

Modesto is in Stanislaus County, which brings in $1.3 billion for California in agricultural production each year.

Rivers

Two great river systems drain this broad valley. The Sacramento River comes in from the north. It enters the valley near Mount Shasta and flows southwest to the San Francisco Bay. Along the way, smaller, swifter rivers feed into the Sacramento River. These rivers include the Yuba, the Feather, and the American.

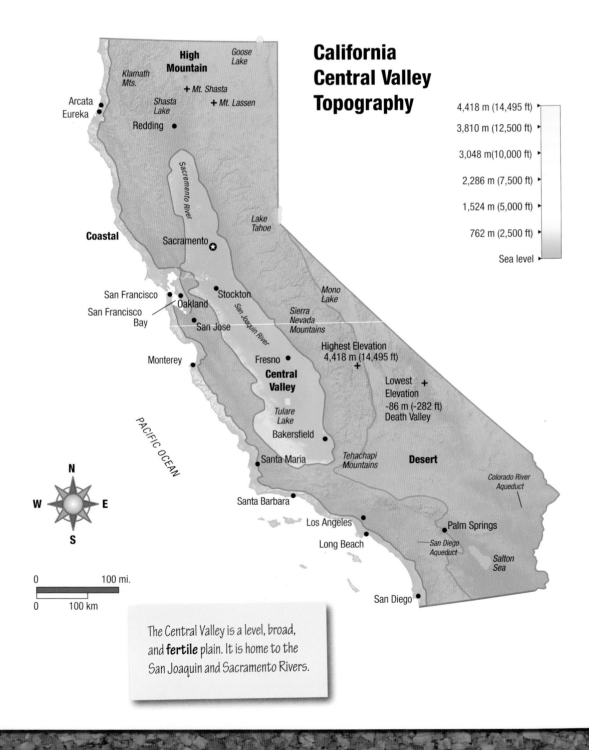

California Central Valley Topography

4,418 m (14,495 ft) ▸
3,810 m (12,500 ft) ▸
3,048 m (10,000 ft) ▸
2,286 m (7,500 ft) ▸
1,524 m (5,000 ft) ▸
762 m (2,500 ft) ▸
Sea level ▸

Goose Lake
High Mountain
Klamath Mts.
+ Mt. Shasta
Arcata
Eureka
Shasta Lake
+ Mt. Lassen
Redding
Sacramento River
Lake Tahoe
Coastal
Sacramento
San Francisco
Stockton
Oakland
Mono Lake
San Francisco Bay
San Jose
San Joaquin River
Sierra Nevada Mountains
Highest Elevation 4,418 m (14,495 ft) +
Monterey
Fresno
Central Valley
Lowest + Elevation -86 m (-282 ft) Death Valley
Tulare Lake
Bakersfield
PACIFIC OCEAN
Santa Maria
Tehachapi Mountains
Desert
Colorado River Aqueduct
Santa Barbara
Los Angeles
Palm Springs
Long Beach
San Diego Aqueduct
Salton Sea
San Diego

N
W   E
S

0   100 mi.
0   100 km

The Central Valley is a level, broad, and **fertile** plain. It is home to the San Joaquin and Sacramento Rivers.

Another set of roaring streams drains into the San Joaquin River system in the south. The San Joaquin River used to flow northwest and empty into the San Francisco Bay. Then, in the 1940s, too many **canals** began to draw water from it. Today, most of its water flows away into farms and fields, and some of its water joins the Sacramento River.

Farmlands near the Sacramento River Valley benefit from nearby water and a good growing **climate**.

Irrigation machinery waters large fields by rolling across the land and spraying water.

California Water Plan

The California Water Plan is an **irrigation** system that carries water from man-made lakes north of the valley to farms at the southern end. Built in the 1960s, the **aqueducts**, canals, and dams move more water than any other system in the world.

Climate

Summers in the Central Valley get extremely hot. Cool ocean breezes do not reach this area. Stockton can reach 38° Celsius (100° Fahrenheit) on a day when San Francisco, just 60 miles to the west, barely reaches 27° Celsius (80° Fahrenheit). By July, only the **irrigated** lands in the valley look green. Everything else has turned golden brown.

Fall is short. Winter comes suddenly. A heavy ground mist called **tule fog** creeps over the Central Valley. Walking through tule fog is like flying through a cloud, because this fog may be 305 meters (1,000 feet) thick. Sometimes **tule fog** covers the entire Valley from Redding to Bakersfield. The Central Valley never gets snow, even though temperatures do sometimes drop below freezing.

Farming

People are drawn to this area because of its rich soil. It is a mixture of sand, clay, and **silt**. Sand makes the soil airy. Clay helps it to hold water. Silt provides the food plants need to grow.

California's silt was built up over countless years by its two great river systems. The richness of the soil has led people to reshape the landscape. Lakes and **marshes** that once dotted the valley have been drained to create farms. The rivers in this region no longer follow the course set by nature. They have all been changed to meet the needs of farmers.

Farming is a big business in the Central Valley. Once owned by families, the **industry** has expanded to become **agribusiness**, run by large companies. Agribusiness companies use machines to plow, to plant, and to grow a wide variety of crops. They produce nuts such as almonds and walnuts. They grow apricots, avocados, grapes, olives, and other fruits. They grow vegetables such as Brussels sprouts, lettuce, artichokes, and herbs such as garlic.

When the crops ripen, machines are unable to pick them properly. **Migrant** workers do this job. Migrant workers move into an area when there is work and move on when the work is done. Many of California's migrants are people from Mexico.

Many cities in the Central Valley serve as farming **hubs**. Crops come into cities such as Fresno and Modesto from surrounding farms. Here, they are packaged for sale or made into products.

California is the leading agricultural state in the United States. Many of the products are grown in the Central Valley.

Central Valley California Resources

Natural Resources	Industry
Oil	Forest products
Natural gas	Fruit
Borax	Grapes
Limestone	Rice
Gold, silver	Vegetables
Sand, gravel	Olives
Manufacturing	Dairy products
Computers	Cotton
Clothing	Sugar beets
	Cattle
	Walnuts
	Poultry
	Fish
	Skiing

Mineral Resources

Petroleum and natural gas are important natural **resources** in the Central Valley. Both **minerals** are pumped out of the ground in the southern part of the Valley. Oil wells and **refineries** can be seen from Bakersfield to Stockton.

Natural gas in the Valley differs from that of southern California. In southern California, gas and oil are usually found together. This is called wet gas. In the Valley, however, natural gas is often found by itself. This so-called dry gas is the more useful type. It is used to fuel furnaces, water heaters, and stoves.

Sacramento: The State Capital

The biggest city in the Valley revolves around quite a different business. Sacramento is the **capital** of California. It buzzes with the business of the state government. The state **capitol** and other government buildings form its center.

Sacramento was born around 1850, as a supply center for gold rush **miners**.

Old Sacramento State Historic Park is home to gold rush-era buildings that still look as they did back then.

The High Mountains

The Sierra Nevada Mountains are like a wall along 644 kilometers (400 miles) of the state's eastern border. The range has more than 500 peaks taller than 3,658 meters (12,000 feet). The highest one, Mt. Whitney, touches the clouds at (4,418 meters) 14,495 feet above sea level. The only higher mountain in the United States is Alaska's Mt. McKinley.

The mountains continue north of the Sierra Nevada, but they belong to a different range called the Cascades. The Cascades were formed by hot liquid rock bursting out of the earth and piling up. The Cascades are actually a string of volcanoes from northern California to Canada. The biggest ones in California are Mount Shasta and Mount Lassen.

Plate movements also created tall mountains in the north. The Klamath Range and Trinity Alps stretch from the Cascades to the coast.

Mt. Whitney is located in Sequoia National Park, east of Fresno.

Snow in California?

Moist air from the ocean cools suddenly when it meets the high mountains and slides upward. The moisture then drops as rain or snow. On the western slopes of the Sierra, the snow can pile up to 15 meters (50 feet) deep in winter. The eastern slopes hardly get any rain or snow, because the air is dry by the time it gets there.

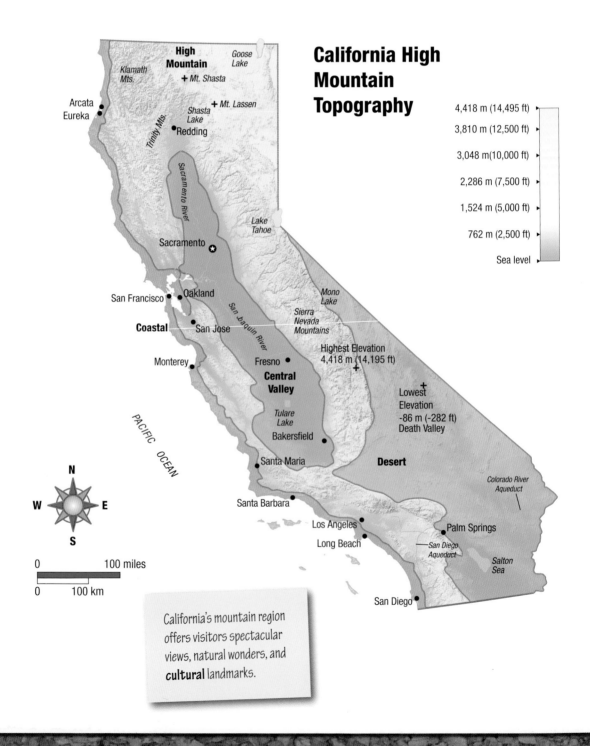

California High Mountain Topography

4,418 m (14,495 ft) ►
3,810 m (12,500 ft) ►
3,048 m (10,000 ft) ►
2,286 m (7,500 ft) ►
1,524 m (5,000 ft) ►
762 m (2,500 ft) ►
Sea level ►

High Mountain
Goose Lake
Klamath Mts.
+ Mt. Shasta
Arcata
Eureka
+ Mt. Lassen
Trinity Mts.
Shasta Lake
Redding
Sacramento River
Lake Tahoe
Sacramento
Oakland
San Francisco
Mono Lake
Coastal
San Jose
Sierra Nevada Mountains
San Joaquin River
Highest Elevation 4,418 m (14,195 ft)
Monterey
Fresno
Central Valley
Lowest Elevation -86 m (-282 ft) Death Valley
Tulare Lake
Bakersfield
PACIFIC OCEAN
Santa Maria
Desert
Colorado River Aqueduct
Santa Barbara
Los Angeles
Palm Springs
Long Beach
San Diego Aqueduct
Salton Sea
San Diego

N W E S

0   100 miles
0   100 km

California's mountain region offers visitors spectacular views, natural wonders, and **cultural** landmarks.

Winters are cold in the mountains. Rain in the valley usually means snow in the mountains. On the other hand, in the summer, when the **foothills** and valley are very hot, the mountains remain pleasantly cool. Not too many people live in the mountains, but thousands go there for **recreation**. Downhill skiing, snowboarding, snowmobiling, hiking, backpacking, hunting, and camping are all popular outdoor activities.

Desperate For Water

The mountains provide more than fun in California. They provide life itself in the form of water. California usually gets no rain in the summer. Most of what falls in the winter runs off into the sea. The state depends on the snowpack in the mountains. The melting of this snow year-round creates rushing streams and rivers.

The rivers in the high mountains have all been **dammed** to create **reservoirs**. Cities all over the state get their drinking water from these reservoirs. Hetch Hetchy, for example, supplies San Francisco. Lake Berryessa supplies cities in the Valley. Los Angeles gets water from Mono Lake and from other lakes.

Shasta Dam, shown here, has enough concrete to build a three-foot-wide sidewalk around the world at the **equator**.

Farmers also need the water for their fields. The cities want more for their ever-growing **suburbs**. Scientists, however, worry about life forms that die when dams are built and lands are flooded.

California High Mountain Resources

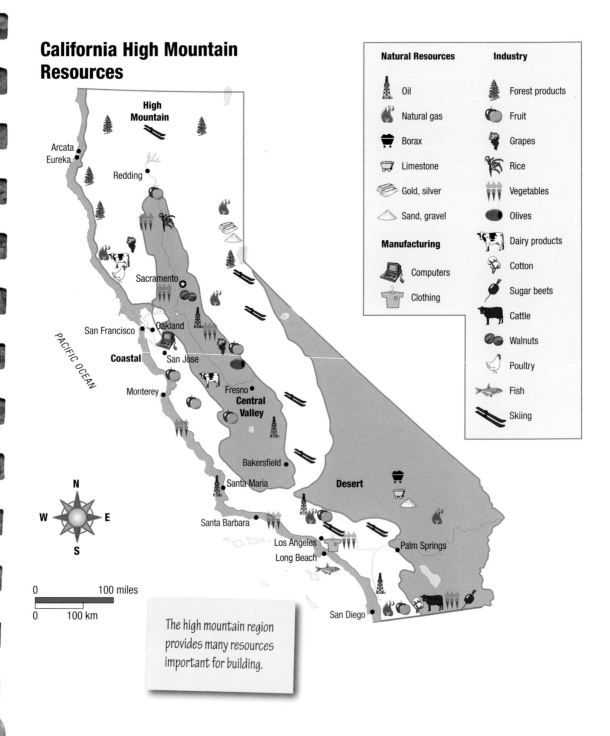

Natural Resources	Industry
Oil	Forest products
Natural gas	Fruit
Borax	Grapes
Limestone	Rice
Gold, silver	Vegetables
Sand, gravel	Olives
Manufacturing	Dairy products
Computers	Cotton
Clothing	Sugar beets
	Cattle
	Walnuts
	Poultry
	Fish
	Skiing

The high mountain region provides many resources important for building.

Trees

Trees are a major natural **resource** of the mountains. Timber brings in a lot of money. Giant redwood trees and Douglas firs cover the northern mountains and the western Sierra. Builders frame most wooden houses out of fir, so this wood is sold for a good price. Redwood has great value, too, because it does not easily rot when it gets wet. Decks, porches, and outdoor furniture are often made of redwood.

More than 90 percent of the original redwoods in California have been cut down by loggers.

Vacation Places

In the Gold Country of the Sierra foothills, gold mining towns like Sonora have been **restored**. Staying in these places is like living during the gold rush days.

Lake Tahoe calls itself the "jewel of the Sierra." It is a popular vacation place. Towns surrounding the lake are filled with shops and restaurants. Attractions include the lake itself, ski areas, and **gambling** in Nevada.

Lake Tahoe straddles the border of Nevada and California. It measures 34 kilometers (21 miles) from tip to tip and 19 kilometers (12 miles) across.

Desert and Basin

In one way, the landscape south of the Sierra is all the same: very dry and hot. Yet it offers great variety, too, with rocky ridges, sudden canyons, dry lake beds, and sandy **basins**.

Death Valley

The California desert may be divided into three areas: Death Valley, the Mojave Desert, and the Colorado Desert. Death Valley occupies the northeastern corner of this region. It is a deep canyon 225 kilometers (140 miles) long and up to 26 kilometers (16 miles) wide. It formed when a chunk of the earth's crust broke and sank.

During the gold rush, some travelers tried to enter California through Death Valley. Many died of thirst while crossing this blazing hot valley. The survivors named it Death Valley.

Mojave and Colorado Deserts

South of Death Valley lies the Mojave Desert. Small mountains break up the flat, sandy landscape. Long ago, the Mojave was part of the Pacific Ocean, but the rising coast range cut it off and turned it into a huge lake. Over time, the water **evaporated**, leaving dry lake beds and salty soil.

The Joshua tree has become a symbol of the Mojave Desert. It is able to survive in an area where most types of plant life cannot.

California Desert Topography

4,418 m (14,495 ft) ►
3,810 m (12,500 ft) ►
3,048 m (10,000 ft) ►
2,286 m (7,500 ft) ►
1,524 m (5,000 ft) ►
762 m (2,500 ft) ►
Sea level ►

Goose Lake

High Mountain

Arcata
Eureka
Shasta Lake
Redding

Sacramento River

Lake Tahoe

Sacramento

Mono Lake

San Francisco   Oakland

Coastal   San Jose

San Joaquin River

Highest Elevation
4,418 m (14,495 ft)
+

Death Valley
+
Lowest Elevation
-86 m (-282 ft)

Monterey   Fresno

Central Valley

Tulare Lake
Bakersfield

PACIFIC   OCEAN

Santa Maria

Desert   Mojave Desert

Colorado River Aqueduct

N
W   E
S

0   100 miles
0   100 km

Santa Barbara

Los Angeles   Palm Springs
Long Beach   San Diego Aqueduct

Salton Sea

Colorado Desert

San Diego

Over 10 million hectares (25 million acres) of California's deserts are publicly owned and include two national parks, one national **preserve**, 6 military bases, 72 wilderness areas, and 14 state parks.

Several small mountain ranges block off the Colorado Desert from the Mojave Desert. The Colorado River runs through the eastern part of the Colorado Desert. The Salton Sea fills its southwestern corner. An **engineer** named Charles Rockwood created this **inland** sea by accident. In 1905 he was building some **irrigation canals** from the Colorado River. A flood broke the banks of one canal. The Colorado River poured into an ancient lake bed for two years, filling it with 25 meters (83 feet) of water. The water cannot drain out, so it keeps getting saltier.

Resources

One might easily think of California's deserts as wastelands. In truth, they are full of valuable **resources**. For example, they have borax, a white salt-like mineral. Borax is an **additive** used to make detergents, gasoline, weed killers, insect killers, glass, and fire extinguishers. California mines over one million tons of borax every year—almost all of the world's supply.

Limestone is also found in the Mojave Desert. This white stone formed out of seashells millions of years ago. It is the key ingredient in Portland cement, made of sand, stone, and water. Portland cement in turn is the key ingredient in concrete. Other ingredients in concrete include sand and gravel. These are also mined by the trainload in the California deserts. By supplying the ingredients for concrete, the deserts have made a big difference to California. Concrete is necessary in almost every structure that is built, from skyscrapers to swimming pools.

Unlike other California deserts, the soil of the Colorado Desert is rich. The Colorado River, one of the biggest rivers in the United States, runs through it. Irrigation canals tap its water to serve farms between the Salton Sea and the Mexican border. This area is called the Imperial Valley, and irrigation has made it bloom. Here, Californians grow alfalfa, cotton, fruit, sugar beets, lettuce, and many other crops.

California Desert Resources

Natural Resources
- Oil
- Natural gas
- Borax
- Limestone
- Gold, silver
- Sand, gravel

Manufacturing
- Computers
- Clothing

Industry
- Forest products
- Fruit
- Grapes
- Rice
- Vegetables
- Olives
- Dairy products
- Cotton
- Sugar beets
- Cattle
- Walnuts
- Poultry
- Fish
- Skiing

High Mountain

Arcata
Eureka
Redding

Sacramento
San Francisco
Oakland
San Jose
Coastal
Monterey
Fresno
Central Valley

PACIFIC OCEAN

Bakersfield
Santa Maria
Santa Barbara
Los Angeles
Long Beach
San Diego

Death Valley

Desert
Mojave Desert
Palm Springs
Colorado Desert

N
W   E
S

0   100 miles
0   100 km

The desert and basin areas provide resources, like borax and limestone, which help create other products.

A Desert Paradise

Palm Springs is the largest city in the California desert. It has about 45,000 people, but the population doubles in winter because of visitors. The main **industry** of this **resort** town is **recreation**. Golf courses, off-road driving tours, tennis, rock climbing, and hiking are all available year-round because of the favorable **climate**.

California is a state of great contrasts. Its four geographic regions offer different climates, landscapes, industries, and resources. Each region has met the challenges of its climate and **landforms**, and uses its resources to benefit all regions of California, as well as the rest of the world.

The Givenchy Hotel and Spa in Palm Springs has 2 indoor swimming pools, 22 treatment rooms, a hair salon, a gift shop, and a café.

Map of California

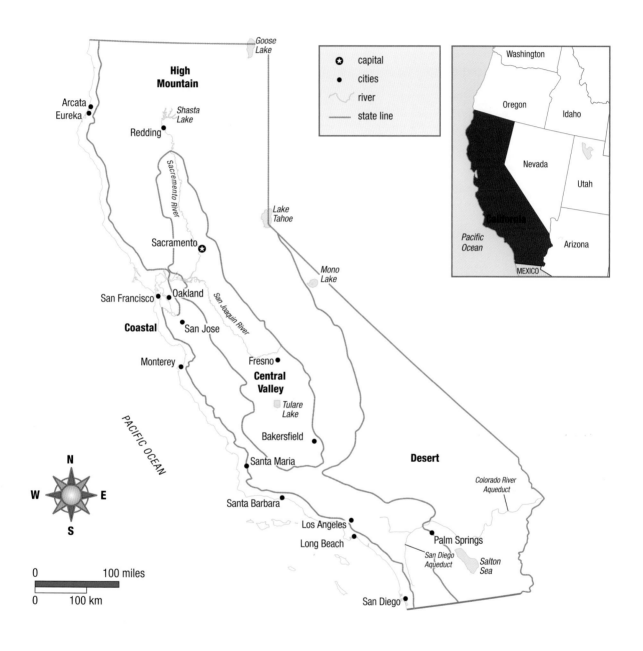

High Mountain

Arcata
Eureka

Goose Lake

Shasta Lake

Redding

Sacramento River

Sacramento ✪

San Francisco ● ●Oakland

Coastal

●San Jose

San Joaquin River

Monterey ●

Fresno ●

Central Valley

Tulare Lake

Bakersfield ●

Santa Maria ●

Santa Barbara ●

Los Angeles ●

Long Beach

San Diego ●

Lake Tahoe

Mono Lake

Desert

Colorado River Aqueduct

● Palm Springs

San Diego Aqueduct

Salton Sea

PACIFIC OCEAN

N
W — **E**
S

| 0 | 100 miles |
| 0 | 100 km |

✪ capital
● cities
river
—— state line

Washington

Oregon
Idaho

Nevada
Utah

California

Pacific Ocean

Arizona

MEXICO

45

Glossary

additive substance added to another in small amounts

agribusiness industry related to farming

aqueduct structure that carries water a long distance

basin area of land drained by a river and its branches

bay window window or set of windows that sticks out from the wall of a building

bioscience study of plants, animals, and other living things

campus grounds of a university or other school

canal artificial waterway

capital center of an industry; location of a government

capitol building in which the legislature meets

climate weather conditions that are usual for a certain area

cultural relating to the ideas, skills, arts, and a way of life of a certain people at a certain time

dammed having a barrier to hold back the flow of water

design to plan a thing to be made or built

development (housing) area of land with houses on it

diverse having variety

economy/economic means of bringing money to a region

engineer person who has charge of an engine or of machinery or technical equipment

equator imaginary circle around the Earth everywhere equally distant from the North and South Poles

ethnic belonging to a group with a particular culture

evaporate to change into a vapor

fertile bearing crops or vegetation in abundance

fertilizer material added to soil to make it more fertile

foothill low hills at the base of a mountain or mountain range

gable triangular part of an outside wall of a building formed by the sides of the roof sloping down

gambling playing a game in which something is risked

hub center of activity

industry group of businesses that offer a similar product or service

inland not near the sea coast

irrigate/irrigation supply water to land

landform natural feature of a land surface

Latino person from a Latin American country or who speaks Spanish; the term Hispanic is also sometimes used to describe such a person

marsh area of soft wet land usually overgrown with grasses and related plants

migrant farm laborer from another country who comes to work in the United States during a growing season

miner person who works in a mine

mineral solid substance formed in the earth by nature and obtained by mining

monorail single rail serving as a track for a wheeled vehicle

peninsula piece of land extending into a body of water

preserve keep or save from injury or ruin

profitable making money

recreation/recreational means of refreshing the mind and body

refinery place with machinery used to bring metals, oil, or sugar to a pure state